Silk Painting
made easy

Silk Painting
made easy

Series Editors: Susan & Martin Penny

David & Charles

A DAVID & CHARLES BOOK

First published in hardback the UK in 1998
First published in paperback in the UK 2003

Distributed in North America
by F&W Publications, Inc.
4700 E. Galbraith Rd.
Cincinnati, OH 45236
1-800-289-0963

ISBN 0 7153 1502 1 (paperback)

Series Editors: Susan & Martin Penny • Designed by Penny & Penny • Illustrations: Fred Fieber at Red Crayola
Photography: Ashton James; Jon Stone • Stylist: Susan Penny

Printed in Italy by Stige SpA
for David & Charles
Brunel House Newton Abbot Devon

David & Charles books are available from all good bookshops.
In case of difficulty, write to us at David & Charles *Direct*, PO Box 6, Newton Abbot,
TQ12 2DW quoting reference M001, or call our credit card hotline on 01626 334555.

Visit our website at www.davidandcharles.co.uk

Contents

Introduction to Silk Painting

Silk Painting Made Easy is the complete guide to the craft of silk painting; to produce beautiful paintings on silk, you will first need to learn a little about the paint, and what will happen when it comes into contact with the silk; then all you need is the step-by-step instructions; a steady hand and a little practice

Essential equipment

Below is a list of the essential equipment needed to paint on silk:

- **Frame** – embroidery or silk painting, used to stretch the silk before painting; frames with wooden interchangeable sides are best.
- **Hoop** – embroidery, can be used to stretch silk for smaller projects.
- **Pins** – 3 pronged silk pins or steel tempered drawing pins, used to hold the silk on to the frame.
- **Masking tape** – used to bind the edges of the silk to stop it fraying; wrap around the frame or hoop to stop the paint soaking in; masking silk that you do not want to paint.
- **Paper** – use copier paper to make a tracing of the design.
- **Artist's paintbrush** - used to apply paint to the surface of the silk.
- **Decorator's paintbrush** – used for brushing salt from the surface of the silk.
- **Paint dish** – flat plastic mixing dish.
- **Screw top jars** – used for storing paint.
- **Kitchen paper** – for mopping up spills.
- **Cotton buds** – used for removing paint from the surface of the silk.
- **Synthetic sponge** – used to make stamps for applying paint to the silk.
- **Thick plastic sheet** – used to keep your working surface clean when painting scrunch fabric.
- **Craft knife** – sharp enough to cut a rubber eraser when making a stamp.

Tips for special effects

✔ Use salt on the surface of wet paint to create a 'mottled' effect
✔ A wet cocktail stick or paintbrush can be used to make lighter spots in wet paint
✔ Stamp the silk with a paint/wallpaper paste mix, with stamps cut from sponge or erasers
✔ Use a wet-on-wet technique to blend paint colours together on the silk

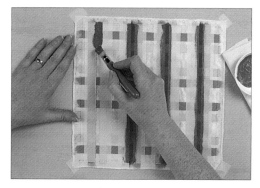

✔ Create a tartan effect on the silk using masking tape and paint to create stripes
✔ Paint fine detail lines on dry background paint to stop them spreading
✔ Apply several paint colours to wet scrunched up silk, for a marbled look

Tips for mounting the silk

✔ Before mounting, bind the edges of the silk or neaten with zig zag stitches
✔ Stretch the fabric as tight as a drum on to the frame or hoop
✔ Any wooden frame that holds the silk taut can be used for silk painting

Tips for painting on silk

✔ Keep your silk stretched 'drum tight' for the best result
✔ Economise by buying the basic paint colours and then mixing your own
✔ Test for gaps in the outliner, before you begin painting. Hold the design up to the light to make sure the line is continuous; if the design is complicated, you may prefer to use a cotton bud and water to wet each area in turn. If there are gaps you will see the water seeping into adjoining areas. Wait until the silk is dry, then mend the gaps. When the outliner is dry, re-test
✔ Do not apply paint over the outliner; allow the paint to spread out to the resist lines

Tips for fixing silk

✔ Leave the paint to dry completely before removing it from the frame
✔ Cover the silk with a cloth before ironing
✔ Iron on a cotton setting for 7 minutes
✔ After fixing wash the silk, then re-iron

Types of silk

✔ Habutai is the best silk for beginners
✔ Habutai comes in three weights: light, medium and heavy
✔ Silk chiffon, silk georgette, silk satin, silk taffata and silk twill can be used for painting
✔ Tear silk, rather than cutting it to get a straight edge
✔ Always test silk before painting, to see how the outliner and the paint will react
✔ Light-weight silk is ideal for scarfs, wall hangings, cards; medium-weight is suitable for clothing
✔ Silk is sold by the metre (yard); as pre-cut pieces; or ready-made items

Choosing the right paint

To help you understand a little more about the paint and outliner you will be working with, listed below are some of the plus and minus points.

● **Silk paint** – Water-based
  Very easy to use
  Pre-mix the paint or mix on the silk
  Brushes can be washed in water
  Dry in just a few hours
  Iron fix before washing
● **Fabric paint** – Water-based
  Colours can be mixed
  Use on silk, enclosed by masking tape
  Brushes can be washed in water
  Iron fix before washing
● **Resist outliner paste** – Water-based
  Quick and easy to use
  Squeeze the tube like an icing nozzle
  Dries in 3-4 hours
  Makes a very effective barrier for paint

● **Metallic pen**
  Very easy to use
  Available at most stationery stores
  Dries almost instantly
  No mess
  Two thicknesses of tip, 0.8 and 1.2mm
  May need two layers
● **Glitter glue**
  A mixture of glue and glitter
  Sold in a pen-like container with a nozzle
  Can be used straight from the tube
  Use only on silk that will not be washed

Mounting and Fixing

Silk painting need not be an expensive hobby, as very little specialist equipment is needed to produce quite spectacular results. The most important part of silk painting is the preparation: the silk must be stretched as tight as a drum, to avoid the paint settling into the dips and drying to a patchy finish

Preparing fabric

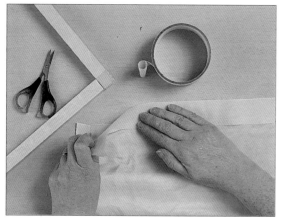

Choose light or medium-weight silk, and always test the paint on the silk before you begin. Bind the edges of the silk with masking tape, or machine zig zag to neaten.

Fixing fabric paint

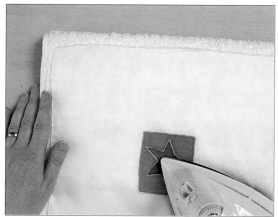

Cover the painted silk with a clean cloth and iron on a cotton setting for 7 minutes to fix the colours. Wash the silk, then iron to remove the creases.

Preparing your frame

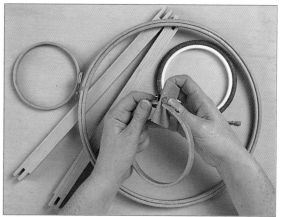

Before you begin painting, the silk needs to be stretched and then raised above your working surface. Choose a frame with wooden interchangeable sides; or for a smaller project use an embroidery hoop. Remove any rough edges with sandpaper.

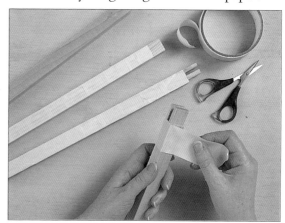

Wrap the frame or hoop with masking tape to stop the paint from soaking into the wood. The masking tape should be wiped or renewed between projects.

Mounting the fabric

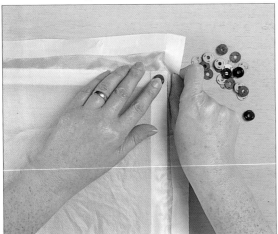

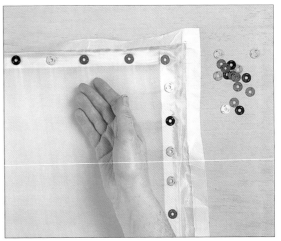

1 The prepared silk should be attached to a wooden frame using 3 pronged silk pins, or steel tempered drawing pins. Stretch the prepared silk over the frame, keeping the grain of the fabric straight. Pin one corner on to the frame, then stretch the silk, while you pin the opposite corner. Fix the other two corners in the same way, pushing the pins firmly into the frame.

3 Repeat the process on the other two sides, again staggering the pins. This will prevent furrows forming on the surface of the silk, which will collect pools of paint. When you have finished pinning all four sides, run the back of your hand over the silk to ensure there are no dips. If the silk is sagging, pull the fabric gently, then add another pin to hold the silk in place.

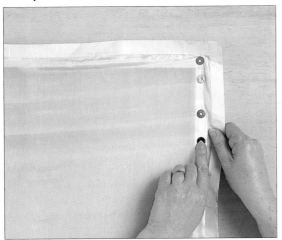

2 Start working down from one top corner. Push a pin into the frame, pulling the silk taut, while keeping the fabric grain straight. Continue working down the side, adding pins about every 5cm (2in). Pin the opposite side tightly, staggering the pins so they are not directly opposite one another.

4 When you are happy with the tightness of the silk you can begin painting. If you are working on a very large project, you may need to raise the frame by placing books under the four corners. This will stop the silk touching your work surface, if it sags under the weight of the wet paint.

Painting Techniques

There are lots of very interesting ways to apply paint to the surface of silk; and lots of different effects that can be achieved with the paint. To contain paint within a design area, it will need to be surrounded by an impenetrable outline. Here we help you explore the different outlining and painting techniques

Making the outlines

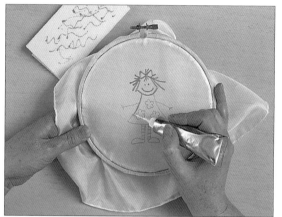

Lay the framed silk over a tracing of the design, then draw over it with a pencil. Use outliner paste to draw over the design lines, keeping an even pressure on the tube. The lines should be continuous or the paint will seep into other areas. Allow 3-4 hours to dry.

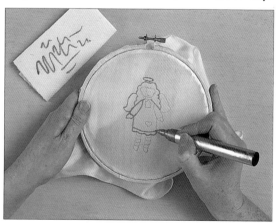

A metallic marker pen can be used to draw the outlines. Test the pen to make sure it is an effective barrier for the paint. The ink will dry almost immediately.

Mixing the paint

Use paint straight from the pot; or blend colours in a dish, using water to lighten the colours. Always mix enough to complete the project, storing in a screw top jar.

Painting the silk

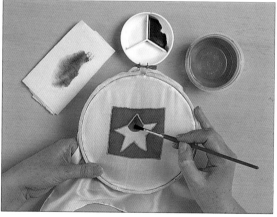

Drop a small amount of paint on to the silk. The paint will spread out to the resist lines, then stop. Add more paint until the area is filled completely with colour.

Mixing colours on the silk

Use the wet-on-wet technique to blend colours together on the silk: dampen the silk before dropping the paint colours next to each other, so they merge together. You will achieve a different effect if you drop paint colours on to dry fabric: the colours will be stronger, and they will merge less.

Water techniques

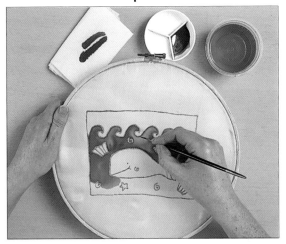

Water can be used to make spots or lighter areas in the paint. Touch the wet paint on the silk with a clean damp paintbrush or cotton bud to pick up some of the paint, while leaving a little water on the surface; or drag the brush over the wet paint to create lighter lines or swirls.

Adding detail to dry paint

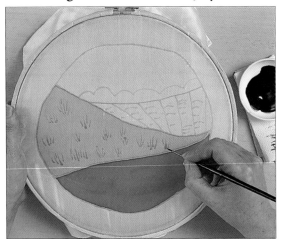

Paint the silk with the background paint colour, then leave to dry. Put a small amount of pure undiluted paint in a dish, leave until a skin begins to form on the paint. Load a fine dry brush with paint. Remove most of it on kitchen paper, before painting fine lines on the silk.

Adding detail to wet paint

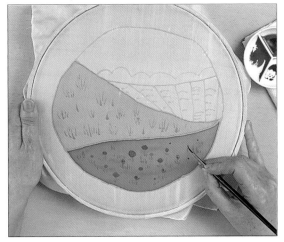

Flower heads can be made by dotting a small amount of pure undiluted paint on to a painted background, allowing the paint to spread across the silk. The background paint should be allowed to dry a little, before adding the second colour; if the background paint is too wet, the colours will merge.

Salt effect

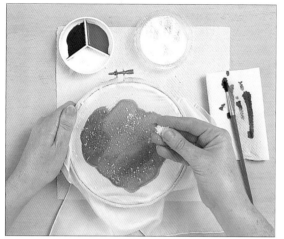

Outline the design area with outliner paste, then paint the silk with one or more colours of silk paint. Sprinkle salt liberally on to the surface of the wet paint – any coarse salt will do, or buy special salt from a silk paint supplier. The salt will act like a sponge soaking-up the paint, leaving water-marks over the surface of the paint. Keep the silk flat, while the paint is drying.

Once the paint has dried, and this may take several hours, use a large dry brush to remove the salt from the surface of the silk. The paint surface will be mottled in appearance. Add any painted detail before using an iron to fix the paint. Wash the fabric to remove any salt residue. Leave to dry then iron.

Scrunch effect

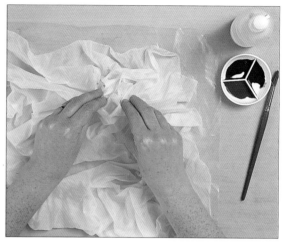

Wet the silk fabric thoroughly with water, then lay it on a sheet of plastic. Scrunch the fabric evenly with your hands. Shake the paint, then put a small amount of each colour into a separate jam jar. Dilute with water: the more water you add the less dense the colour will be. Shake the paint until the colours are thoroughly mixed together, then pour into a dish.

Drop the paint randomly on to the silk using a brush, allowing the colours to mingle, until no white silk remains. Add extra sparkle to the fabric by spraying with gold fabric paint mixed with a little water. Leave the silk to dry before removing it from the plastic and ironing to fix the paint.

Wallpaper paste resist

When stamping with fabric paint on to silk, mix the paint with wallpaper paste powder, this will thicken the paint, making it act like a resist, stopping the paint from spreading across the fabric. Use about 1/2 teaspoon of dry wallpaper paste to approximately 50mls of paint. Before you begin stamping, test the paint on a spare piece of silk fabric.

Use a brush to load the stamp with thickened paint, then press the stamp flat on to the fabric. Leave the paint to dry completely, then wash the fabric to remove the paste mixture. If the colour washes away add more paint to the mix; if the paint bleeds across the fabric, add more paste. Iron fix the fabric.

Using a masking tape grid

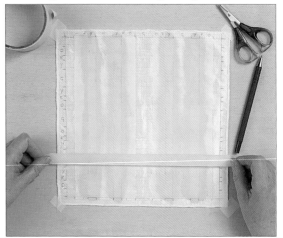

To create a tartan effect: plan the design on paper, before marking the outer edge of the silk to show the position of the masking tape strips. Add the initial letters of each paint colour on to the edge of the fabric. Position the tape between the vertical marks, for the first paint colour. Apply the paint between the tape strips. Leave to dry, then remove the tape.

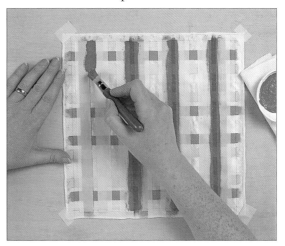

Use a dabbing motion to apply the paint, working just over the edges of the masking tape on either side of the strip. Paint the vertical then the horizontal stripes, masking, painting then removing the tape before moving on to the next colour. Leave the paint to dry before using an iron to fix the colours.

Happy Whale

This delightful underwater scene has been painted in bright colours, capturing the spirit and the heat of the Mediterranean. Fish, shells and starfish bob along in the current, while a large pink whale frolics contentedly in the warm blue water

You will need

- Medium-weight silk – 1.3mx40cm (1⅜ydx15in)
- Lightweight iron-on interfacing – 52x40cm (20x15in)
- Cushion pad – 30cm (12in) square
- Silk paint – deep blue, raspberry pink, buttercup yellow, meadow green, mandarin orange, aqua blue
- Resist outliner paste – gold
- Embroidery or silk painting frame, masking tape, pins
- Matching thread
- Soft pencil
- Paintbrush, scissors
- Container of clean water, kitchen paper
- White paper, double-sided tape
- Iron, fluffy towel, clean cloth
- Sewing machine

Preparing the fabric

1 From the silk cut two pieces 36x36cm (14x14in) for the cushion front and back, and one piece 52x40cm (20x15in) from the triangular border edging, adding extra fabric for mounting on to a frame. Press the silk then attach the cushion front to a frame (see Mounting and Fixing, page 8).

2 Make a tracing of the cushion front on page 18 and 19. Trace the centre panel, then add the corners by turning or flipping the corner section as shown in the diagram on page 19. Place the tracing, with the design facing upwards, underneath the stretched silk and secure in position with small pieces of masking tape.

3 Trace the design on to the silk, using a soft pencil. If you feel confident enough you could apply the outliner directly to the silk over the tracing. Make sure that the lines are continuous as any gaps will allow the paint to seep through. Remove the design, and re-tighten the silk if necessary.

4 Use the gold resist outliner to draw over the outlines of each design. Squeeze the tube gently keeping your hand steady, as if using an icing tube. Always keep the kitchen paper to hand and whenever you stop, wipe the nozzle and replace the cap. Take care to keep

the lines continuous as any gaps will allow the paint to seep through. Leave the outliner to dry for 3-4 hours before painting.

Applying the fabric paint

1 When using silk paint, drop a small amount of paint on to the fabric with a fine paintbrush. The paint will spread out to the resist lines, then stop. Add more paint until the area is filled completely with colour.

2 Fill the area above the whale with aqua blue paint. To achieve the spotty effect: touch the wet paint with a clean damp paintbrush. The paintbrush will soak-up some of the paint, while making a lighter spot on the paint (see Painting Techniques, page 11).

3 The area behind the whale is filled, as above, with the deep blue paint. Using a wetter brush, make large water spots, following the technique above. While the paint is still wet, use a clean damp brush, or a damp cotton bud to soak-up some of the paint colour on either side of the resist lines, along both sides of the waves.

4 Paint the whale using raspberry pink, adding water spots. Use the main photograph on page 15 to complete the design. Leave the paint to dry.

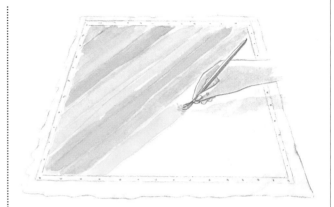

5 Mount the silk for the cushion back on to a frame. Load a clean brush with meadow green paint and then add a little water to the brush. Paint the first stripe on the fabric. Clean the brush then apply the buttercup yellow and then the mandarin orange in the same way across the fabric. The wet paint will stop when it meets the edge of the next wet colour, then merge, forming a soft watercolour effect. Repeat the stripes until the fabric is covered. Allow to dry before removing the painted silk from the frame.

6 Mount the silk fabric to be used for the triangular border on to a frame. Using the outliner paste, draw across the fabric, dividing it into three equal sections, widthways. Leave the resist to dry for 3-4 hours. Use green, yellow and orange to paint each of the three sections a different colour. Leave the silk to dry before removing it from the frame.

Fixing the paints

1 Lay the painted fabric on a fluffy towel and cover with a clean cotton cloth, iron for about 7 minutes on a cotton setting. Fix all three pieces of fabric in this way.

Making the triangular border

1 Iron interfacing on to the back of the striped backing fabric.

2 Make a template of the triangle on page 19 on to white paper with a soft pencil. Cut out the template, then lay it on to the fabric. Draw around the edge using a soft pencil.

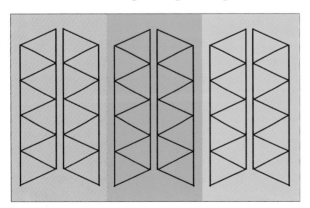

From each colour you will need to cut 16 triangles. To do this: turn the triangular template, facing alternately up and down across each strip of colour.

3 Cut out the triangles, then place them in twos, right sides together. Pin and stitch, using a 3mm (¹/₈in) seam allowance, around the top two sides. Clip the seam allowance, then turn each triangle to its right side, press flat.

Assembling the cushion cover

1 Lay six triangles on to each side of the cushion front. Position the triangles so that their points face towards the centre of the

cushion; match the raw edges of the cushion with the raw edges of each triangle. Pin, tack then machine stitch 1cm (³⁄₈in) in from the edge.

2 Place the cushion back, with right sides facing, on top of the cushion front. The triangles should be sandwiched between the two layers. Pin, tack and machine stitch 1.5cm (⁵⁄₈in) in from the fabric edge along all four

sides, leaving an opening of 15cm (6in) in the middle of one edge. Neaten the seam then turn through to the right side. Press the cover, then insert the cushion pad and close the opening with small neat stitches.

If you want to paint the picture, as shown on page 14, trace just the central part of the whale design, shown below.

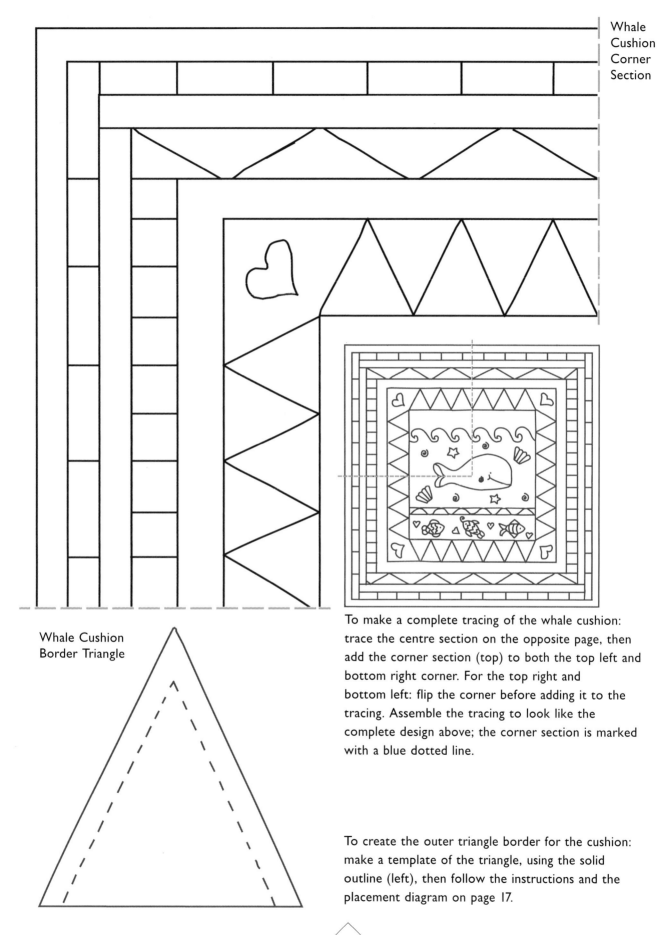

Whale
Cushion
Corner
Section

Whale Cushion
Border Triangle

To make a complete tracing of the whale cushion: trace the centre section on the opposite page, then add the corner section (top) to both the top left and bottom right corner. For the top right and bottom left: flip the corner before adding it to the tracing. Assemble the tracing to look like the complete design above; the corner section is marked with a blue dotted line.

To create the outer triangle border for the cushion: make a template of the triangle, using the solid outline (left), then follow the instructions and the placement diagram on page 17.

Daisy Chain

Pretty daisy-like flowers have been used to decorate the top of this pine box, which has been brought right up-to-date by dragging it with a wash of blue paint. Then, when the weather is bad and you stay indoors and stitch, the box will be a constant reminder of warm sunny days spent in the garden

You will need

- Lightweight silk – 46x15cm (18x6in)
- Silk paint – orange, yellow, amethyst
- Resist outliner paste – pearl gold
- Card mount – aperture size 9.5x7cm (3¾x2¾in)
- Gift tag – 3.5cm (1½in) square
- Wooden trinket box – aperture 14x9.5cm (5½x3¾in)
- Thin wadding
- Embroidery ring or silk painting frame
- White paper, double-sided tape, pins
- All-purpose glue
- Soft pencil, masking tape
- Container of clean water, kitchen paper
- Scissors
- Paintbrushes
- Iron, fluffy towel, clean cloth

Tracing the design

1 Cut a piece of silk large enough to take all the designs; or smaller pieces for individual cards or the box top, adding extra fabric for mounting on to the frame. Press the silk then attach it to a silk painting frame; or stretch across an embroidery ring (see Mounting and Fixing, page 8).

2 Make a tracing of the designs on page 23 on to white paper using a soft pencil. For the card design: use either daisy and a section of the background grid. Place the tracing, with the design facing upwards, underneath the stretched silk and secure in position with small pieces of masking tape.

3 Trace the design on to the silk, using a soft pencil. Remove the paper tracing, and re-tighten the silk if necessary.

Applying the outliner

1 If you feel confident enough using resist outliner paste, you could work directly on to the silk without drawing the pencil outlines first; or apply the pearl gold resist outliner over the outlines of the daisy centres and petals. Squeeze the tube gently, as if using an icing tube, and whenever you stop, wipe the nozzle and replace the cap. Take care to keep the lines continuous as any gaps will allow the paint to seep through.

Sheep Scarf and Picture

This delightful rural scene is painted using a variety of colours, techniques and breeds of sheep. The grid of fields can be reduced or enlarged to fit a pocket handkerchief or a large bedspread; so why not get painting, then you can spend the night beneath rolling hills, counting sheep

Ready-made silk scarfs are available from most good craft suppliers, or you could make your own: cut a square of silk fabric, roll the edges, holding in place with small neat stitches. The grid of fields can be used on any size of fabric.

You will need

- Silk scarf – 74cm (29in) square
- Silk handkerchief 28cm (11in) square
- Resist outliner paste – black, clear
- Silk paint – apple green, dark green, yellow, ochre, blue, red, brown
- Coarse salt
- Water soluble fabric marking pen
- Silk painting frame, pins, masking tape
- Fine watercolour brush for grass strokes
- Fine and medium brushes for sheep
- Large brush
- Screw top jars, flat dish and teaspoon for mixing paint, container of clean water, kitchen paper
- White paper, glue, scissors
- Iron, fluffy towel, clean cloth

Planning your design

1 The sheep are designed to be placed randomly over the fields; or they can be placed in family groups or flocks, using as few or as many as you like.

2 Trace the sheep and lambs on page 29; use them as they are or reverse the tracing to have some of the animals facing in the other direction. If you want to plan the design more carefully: mark an area the same size as the fabric on a large piece of paper then, using the instructions given below for setting out the fields, draw the field lines on to the paper plan. On a separate sheet of paper, trace as many sheep as you need to fill the design. Cut out the sheep and glue in position on the plan.

Marking out the fields

1 Mount the silk scarf on to the silk painting frame (see Mounting and Fixing, page 8). Divide one side of the scarf into six equal parts. Mark these divisions, with small lines, on to the side of the scarf using a water soluble pen. Mark the other sides in the same way.

2 Following the diagram on the next page, and using the water soluble pen, join up the marks A-A, B-B, C-C working across the scarf. Finally, join lines D-D and E-E, starting and finishing approximately one sixth in from each side.

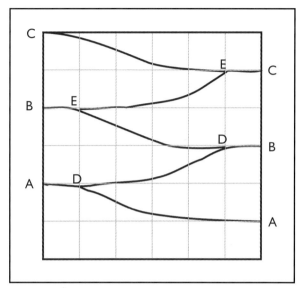

3 Draw freehand wavy lines for rows of hedges and trees, using the diagram above and on page 29 as a guide.

4 Position the traced sheep under the silk fabric and, using a water soluble pen, draw their outlines on to the fabric.

Applying the outliner

1 Using black outliner paste, draw over all the design lines of the sheep and lambs. Keep an even pressure on the tube, which will make the line of an even thickness. It is important that the line is continuous or the paint will seep on to an adjoining area of fabric (see Painting Techniques, page 10).

2 Using clear outliner paste, draw in the field and tree outlines, making sure the lines do not cross over the sheep, or on to the tree shapes. Using the clear outliner draw rough lines across Field 3 to give a ploughed effect. Leave the outliner to dry for 3-4 hours before painting.

Mixing the Paint

1 Mix together the two greens, yellow, and ochre paint to make five or six different

shades of green. For example: lime green, light blue-green, medium blue-green, medium yellow-green, dark blue-green and olive green. Try the colours on a scrap of silk, thinning with water if required. Mix up large enough quantities to paint each field, then store in screw top jars.

Using silk paint

1 In this design there are four types of field: plain, salt effect, ploughed, and with painted grass and flowers. Use a large brush for the plain areas, and a medium brush around the sheep, sweeping the paint close to the sheep then allowing it to flow up to their outline.

Painting the fields

1 Field 1 – red flowers
Paint the field with lime green silk paint; then, when almost dry, use a fine paint brush to drop on small spots of red paint – these will spread out to form the flower heads. Allow to dry before adding the grass stalks using a fine brush and darker green paint.

2 Field 2 – salt effect
Paint this field using the salt effect technique (see Painting Techniques, page 12). Paint with dark blue-green silk paint. Sprinkle the salt on to the surface of the wet paint; allow to dry before brushing off the salt. Any coarse salt will do, or buy special salt from the silk paint supplier.

3 Field 3 – ploughed field
Mix the ochre with a little red, or use a brown silk paint for this field. Add a little light green along some of the ploughed lines.

4 Field 4 – blue flowers
Paint the field with light blue-green silk paint; then, when almost dry, use a fine paint

brush to drop on small spots of blue paint – these will spread out to form the flower heads. Allow to dry before adding the grass stalks using a fine brush and a darker green paint (see Paint Techniques, page 11).

5 Field 5 - grass
Paint the field with a medium yellow-green silk paint, adding a few blades of grass when dry.

6 Field 6 – salt effect
Paint this field using the salt effect technique (see Painting Techniques, page 12). Paint with lime green silk paint. Sprinkle salt on to the surface of the wet paint; allow to dry completely before brushing off the salt. If preferred, this field could be turned into an area of sky: use pale blue silk paint, leaving some areas unpainted for clouds.

Painting the trees

1 Trees 1
Paint the bottom row of trees with dark blue-green silk paint.

2 Trees 2
Paint the middle row of trees with dark olive green silk paint. Sprinkle salt on to the surface of the wet paint; allow to dry completely before brushing off the salt.

3 Trees 3
Paint the top row of trees with dark blue-green paint. Sprinkle with salt, leave to dry, then brush off the salt.

Painting the sheep

1 The sheep can be painted in four ways: all white sheep (Dorset Breed), white should be left unpainted; black face, ears and legs, white body (Suffolk breed); patches of black on white; all black with salt effect – for the all black sheep paint the face and legs with a small brush and black paint, then using a medium brush paint the body black. While the paint is still wet, sprinkle salt on to the body of the sheep. Leave to dry then brush off. This will give a woolly effect to the coat.

Finishing touches

1 Once the scarf has dried, you can add some fine decorative details to finish it off.

2 Field 1 – red flowers
Using a very fine brush, paint small spirals of red paint on and around the spots of red already painted on the silk. Add blades of grass to the silk using dark green paint in fine quick strokes. When adding grass to the field, arrange it randomly around the feet of the sheep and close to the mouths of the grazing sheep.

Jewelled Christmas

If you prefer modern Christmas colours, then these designs painted in jewel-like shades of pink and blue, will certainly appeal. The borders are filled with swirls of silver; while in the middle is a heart, crown and star motif. Silver mounts have been use to complete these petite designs

Metallic marker pens are available from all good stationery suppliers. Several thicknesses of tip are usually available: if you are using a finer tip you may have to go over the lines several times to ensure they provide an effective barrier for the paint.

You will need

- Lightweight silk
- Silk paint – violet, blue, mint
- Permanent marker tip size 0.8mm – metallic silver
- Silver square card – 7.5cm (3in) aperture
- Silver gift tags – 4cm (1½in) diameter aperture
- Thin polyester wadding
- Embroidery ring or silk painting frame, masking tape, pins
- Soft pencil
- Paintbrush, scissors
- White paper, double-sided tape
- Iron, fluffy towel, cotton cloth

Tracing the design

1 Cut a piece of silk large enough to take the designs, adding extra fabric for mounting on to a frame. Press the silk then attach it to a the frame, or stretch across an embroidery ring.

2 Make a tracing of the designs on page 33 on to white paper using a soft pencil. Place the tracing, with the design facing upwards, underneath the stretched silk and secure in position with small pieces of masking tape.

3 Trace the design on to the silk, using a soft pencil. Remove the paper tracing, and re-tighten the silk if necessary.

Applying the outlines

1 Test the permanent marker pen on a spare piece of fabric: draw a small circle with the pen, making sure you start and finish from the same point. The pen line should act like a resist outliner, holding back the paint colours. The ink from the metallic pen will dry almost immediately; drop a small amount of paint into the circle using a fine paintbrush, the paint will spread out to the pen lines, then stop. If you find the paint seeps through the line then you are using the wrong type of marker pen.

2 When you are happy with the test: draw over the pencil design lines using the

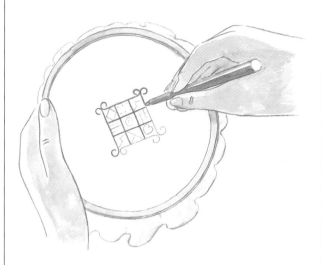

silver permanent marker pen. Draw the outer square first; then the wiggly dividing lines; finally the four motifs and the patterned border.

3 For the gift tags, draw the outlines, then fill in with the motifs and patterns.

Applying the paint

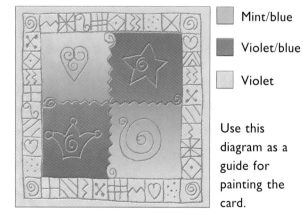

■ Mint/blue

■ Violet/blue

□ Violet

Use this diagram as a guide for painting the card.

1 As the metallic pen dries instantly you can start painting straightaway. Each of the four square sections on the card are painted by merging colours together on the silk. Ensure the first colour is still wet when you apply the second. On two of the squares the mint has been dropped on to one end of the square,

while blue has been dropped on to the other; the centre line of the square then becomes a mix of the two. On the other two squares, the colours are violet and blue. Follow the diagram and key below for placing the colours. Experiment using the paint, as you may prefer to mix a little of the two colours together in a dish before painting the fabric.

2 The border area is filled with violet paint, watered down to give a lighter shade.

3 The gift tags are painted in the same way, merging one colour into another.

4 Remove the fabric from the frame or hoop. Cover with a clean cotton cloth and iron on a medium setting for approximately 7 minutes to fix the colours.

Assembling the designs

1 Use cards and gift tag-cards with pre-cut apertures. Make sure that the painting disappears under the edge of the card or tag. When pre-cut aperture cards are being used, measure the opening and cut the silk 1cm (3/8in) larger all the way around.

2 Use double-sided tape to position the silk centrally inside the aperture. Place a thin piece of polyester wadding at the back of the design and then fold the card over to enclose the silk.

Use these designs to create your own jewelled card and tags.

Seahorse Beach Set

Cut a dash on your next holiday with this charming beach set. Instead of an old plastic bag, use this roomy seahorse bag and sunglasses case to carry those essential little items to the sand. Then when you settle down on your deck chair; your glasses, sun cream and paperback will be close at hand

You will need

- For the bag: lightweight white silk, two pieces 21x28cm (8½x11in) plus extra for mounting on to a frame; felt, two pieces 21x28cm (8½x11in), white; lining fabric, two pieces 21x28cm (8½x11in); thick cord 2m (2¼yd) – turquoise
- For the sunglasses case: lightweight silk, two pieces 12.5x19.5cm (5x8in) plus extra fabric for mounting on to a frame; felt, two pieces 12.5x19.5cm (5x8in); lining fabric, two pieces 12.5x19.5cm (5x8in); heavyweight interfacing, two pieces 12.5x19.5cm (5x8in); thin cord 1m (1⅛yd) – turquoise
- Silk paint – royal blue, deep turquoise, pale greeny turquoise, light green, ochre, orange, yellow
- Sewing thread - to match the painted silk and white
- Outliner paste – clear
- Permanent marker – metallic gold tip size 0.8mm
- Embroidery hoop or silk painting frame, masking tape, pins, soft pencil, scissors
- Paintbrushes, container of clean water
- Iron, fluffy towel, clean cloth

Preparing the fabric

1 Cut a piece of silk fabric large enough for the front and back of both designs; or cut into individual pieces, adding extra for mounting the silk on to a frame. Press the silk then attach it to a frame, or stretch across an embroidery ring (see Mounting and Fixing, page 8).

2 Make tracings of the designs on pages 38 and 39 on to white paper using a soft pencil. Place the tracings, facing upwards, underneath the stretched silk and secure in position with small pieces of masking tape.

3 Trace the designs on to the silk, using a soft pencil. Remove the paper tracing, and re-tighten the silk if necessary.

Outlining the designs

1 Outline the seahorse and starfish for the front of the bag, using the gold marker pen (see Painting Techniques, page 10).

2 Outline the waves and the outer cutting line around each design with clear outliner. Squeeze the tube gently keeping your hand steady, as if using an icing tube. Always keep the kitchen paper to hand and whenever you stop, wipe the nozzle and replace the cap. Take care to keep the lines continuous as any gaps will allow the paint to seep through. Leave the outliner to dry for 3-4 hours.

Mixing the colours

1 Mix the colours in a dish before you begin painting. The reference letters for each colour given below, should be used in conjunction with the diagrams on page 37 when painting. BL – royal blue mixed with a little water to lighten; AZ – deep turquoise mixed with pale greeny turquoise; TQ – pale turquoise straight from the pot; GR – light green mixed with a spot of pale green turquoise; OR – orange mixed with yellow to make a golden orange.

Painting the design

1 When using silk paint, drop a small amount of paint on to the fabric with a fine paintbrush. The paint will spread out to the resist lines, then stop. Add more paint until the area is filled completely with colour.

2 Fill the seahorses with golden orange, then with a fine brush, add a touch of yellow to the face, letting the colours mingle. In the same way add yellow to the nose, back fin tips and along the length of the body and tail.

3 Add ochre to the back of the head, base of fin and down the length of the back and tail, on the opposite side to the yellow.

4 Colour the starfish in the same way using orange first and adding touches of yellow and ochre. Paint the eye centre green.

5 Fill in the waves, following the diagram opposite for colour placement.

6 Add royal blue to the bag at the top and bottom and around the starfish.

7 Paint the front of the bag and sunglasses case. On the back of the bag, paint the waves and the starfish border but omit the seahorses; on the back of the sunglasses case paint only the waves.

Fixing the colour

1 Place the silk painted side down on a fluffy towel, cover with a clean cloth and iron on a cotton setting for approximately 7 minutes to fix the colours.

2 Wash to remove the clear outliner, dry and then iron again.

Making up the bag

1 Pin felt to both the front and back bag pieces. Use white cotton to hand quilt the layers together along every second wave line, using small neat even running stitches.

2 With right sides together, place the lining fabric over one of the pieces of felt-backed silk. Machine stitch, using a seam allowance of 1.5cm (⅝in) along the top edge and 5cm (2in) down each side. Stitch the other piece of felt-backed silk and lining together, then turn right side out.

3 Place the assembled front and back, right sides together. Stitch just the painted silk and felt backing layers together, down the sides and across the bottom, leaving a gap on both sides for the cord.

4 Stitch the lining pieces together, leaving a small gap on one side for turning. The bag and the lining should now be in one piece. Trim the felt close to the stitching.

5 Turn the bag to the right side, through the gap in the lining. Push the lining inside the bag. Sew up the gap in the lining.

6 Make two rows of stitching straight across the bag on both sides to make the channels for the cord. Cut the cord into two lengths and thread one piece through each side. Knot the two ends together on each side.

Making up the sunglasses case

1 Sandwich the felt between the painted silk front and the interfacing, pin the layers together. Repeat for the back.

2 Using white sewing cotton, hand quilt the layers together along the wave lines. Use small neat running stitches working across the fabric on alternate waves.

3 Pin and tack the assembled case, right sides together, along the sides and bottom. Machine stitch, with a 1.5cm (⅝in) seam allowance, down both sides and across the bottom of the case. Leave the top open.

4 Trim off the felt and interfacing close to the stitching. Cut off 1.5cm (⅝in) of felt and interfacing from the top of the case, leaving only the silk.

5 Machine stitch the two lining pieces together, leaving the top edge open.

6 Insert the lining into the case, then turn in the top edge of both the lining and the case. Neatly hand stitch the lining and the case together. Attach the cord around the edge of the bag, making a loop in one corner.

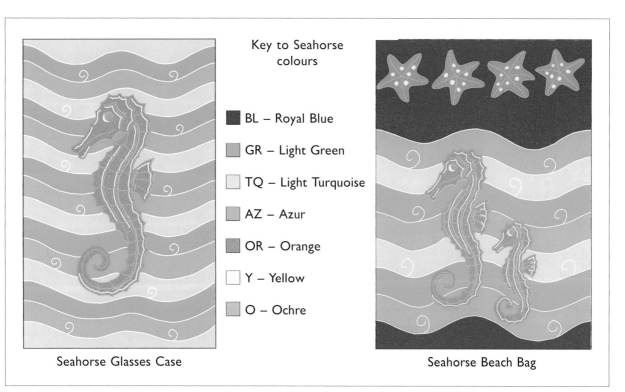

Key to Seahorse colours

BL – Royal Blue
GR – Light Green
TQ – Light Turquoise
AZ – Azur
OR – Orange
Y – Yellow
O – Ochre

Seahorse Glasses Case

Seahorse Beach Bag

Use the design above to make the glasses case: make a tracing of the black lines; the pink lines are the quilting lines, and the blue lines are the seam allowance lines for making-up the bag.

Make a tracing of the bag design on the right, extending the design 1.5cm (⁵⁄₈in) on all sides for the seam allowance; the pink lines are the quilting lines; the blue lines form the cord casing.

Tartan Cushion and Tie-back

Here's a delightful way to co-ordinate your soft furnishings: this cushion and tie-back are painted using a simple masking technique. With a little patience and colour testing, you could create designs to blend with any colour scheme

You will need

- Medium heavyweight ivory silk dupion fabric – 90x112cm (1ydx45in)
- Yellow chintz for cushion back and trim – 70x122cm (³/₄ydx48in)
- Cushion pad – 44x44cm (17x17in)
- Lightweight wadding – 23x122cm (¹/₄ydx48in)
- Fabric paint – two pots yellow, one green, red, white, dark brown
- Sewing thread to match contrast fabric
- Chunky piping cord size No 6 – 1.8m (2yd)
- Brass curtain rings – four x2.5cm (1in)
- Masking tape – 2cm (³/₄in) and 2.5cm (1in)
- Fabric marking pen
- Clean jars, medium stencil brush, flat dish and teaspoon for mixing paint, kitchen paper, container of clean water
- Lining paper, kitchen paper, scissors, ruler
- Sewing machine with zipper foot, pins, needle
- Iron, fluffy towel, clean cloth

Preparing the fabric

1 Press the silk fabric. Using a fabric marking pen, mark on the silk fabric a 47cm (18¹/₂in) square for the cushion and a 24x54.5cm (9¹/₂x21¹/₂in) rectangle for each tie-back. The quantities of fabric given are sufficient to make one 17in (44cm) cushion cover and one pair of curtain tie-backs large enough to hold a double width muslin/lace curtain: for lined curtains or those made from thicker fabric, you will need to lengthen the tie-backs to accommodate the extra thickness of fabric. Do not cut the silk at this stage.

2 At the centre point on one side of the fabric, mark a central stripe 2.5cm (1in) wide for the green paint. The sequence of colours on each side is as follows: green is the central colour, with orange, red, yellow, green, yellow, red, orange repeated outwards towards the corner. The same colours repeat on the other side of the centre. This colour sequence should be marked on each side of the square and rectangular fabric pieces, using a fabric marking pen. The orange stripe should be 1.25cm (¹/₂in) wide, the red stripe 6mm (¹/₄in), the yellow stripe 1.25cm (¹/₂in) and the green stripe 2.5cm (1in). The final stripe will be the width of the remaining fabric. On the edge of the fabric between the pen marks, add the initial letter of each paint colour, following the diagram on page 43.

Glitzy Scrunch Fabric

This stunning silk fabric is very simple to paint, and can be used to make any number of garments. The gold fabric paint will glisten as it catches the light making it rich enough for an evening waistcoat or blouse; any scrap of fabric left over can be used to cover buttons or make a bow-tie

Self-cover buttons are available in a wide range of sizes, from most good haberdashery stores. If you are making the painted silk into a garment, the colour will be enhanced if the silk is backed with a dark coloured lining fabric.

You will need
- Medium-weight silk
- Silk paint – mauve, navy blue, bright blue, gold
- Water
- Plastic sheet
- Spray bottle
- Large paintbrush
- Jam jars, kitchen paper
- Iron, fluffy towel, clean cloth

Applying the design

1 Wet the silk fabric thoroughly with water, then lay it on a sheet of plastic (see Painting Techniques, page 12). Scrunch the fabric evenly with your hands.

2 Shake each paint bottle, then put a small amount of each colour into a separate jam jar. Dilute with water: the more water you add the less dense the colour will be. Mix the water and paint thoroughly.

3 Drop the paint randomly on the silk using a brush, allowing the colours to mingle on the silk, until no white remains.

4 Dilute some gold fabric paint in a spray bottle with water. Shake well then spray over the fabric.

5 Leave the silk to dry completely before removing it from the plastic. To fix the silk paint: place the silk painted side down on a fluffy towel, cover with a clean cloth and iron for 7 minutes on a cotton setting.

6 Once the paint has been fixed, allow the fabric to settle for a couple of days before washing. Wash in hand-hot water using a non-detergent soap. Rinse the silk in warm water and allow to dry. For best results iron while still damp.

Dolly Bag and Picture

Who knows what girls like to keep in a dolly bag? This one is not just dolly by name but also in the charming design, reminiscent of a comic-strip character. Whether you make the bag or just the picture, either will make a lovely gift or a special keepsake

You will need

- For the dolly bag: lightweight silk, three pieces 11x14cm (4¹/₂x5¹/₂in) – add extra fabric to allow for mounting on to a frame
- Pink checked fabric, two pieces 35x31.5cm (14x12¹/₂in) – bag sides
- Yellow fabric, two circles 23.5cm (9¹/₄in) in diameter – bag bottom
- White fabric 35x14cm (14x5¹/₂in) – pocket lining
- Yellow cord for the bag handle – 1m (40in)
- Bias binding 2m (2¹/₄yd) – yellow
- For the picture: lightweight silk, 15x8cm (6x3¹/₄in) – add extra fabric for mounting
- Frame – with a 6x12cm (2³/₈x4³/₄in) aperture
- Polyester wadding – to fit the frame
- For both projects: silk paint – lemon, rose, cyclamen, mint green, blue
- Permanent gold metallic pen – tip size 0.8mm
- Embroidery ring or silk painting frame, masking tape, pins, soft pencil, tracing paper, scissors
- Sewing machine, matching sewing thread
- Paint brush, container of clean water, kitchen paper, iron, clean cloth

Tracing the bag design

1 Cut three pieces of silk for the dolly bag panels, each 11x14cm (4¹/₂x5¹/₂in), adding extra fabric for mounting the silk on to an embroidery ring or frame. Stretch the silk on to a ring or frame (see Mounting and Fixing, page 8). If you want to paint the three panels together, leave the fabric as one piece and mount on to a larger frame.

2 Trace off the designs on page 50 and 51, using the tracing paper. Lay the tracing under the taut silk and trace over the outlines with a soft pencil. Remove the tracing.

Applying the outline

1 The silk paint will be held within the separate areas of the design by the gold outlines. This has been done using a permanent gold metallic marker pen with a tip size of 0.8mm (see Painting Techniques, page 10). Test the pen on a scrap of silk to make sure it will stop the silk paint from spreading across the fabric.

2 Using the gold marker pen draw over the girls, the flowers at each corner and the border outlines. Make sure that the gold outline is continuous and substantial enough to form a complete line leaving no gaps for the paint to seep through. Leave the outline to dry for a few minutes.

3 Using fabric paint and a paint brush, begin filling in the painted areas of the design: load your brush with a small quantity of paint then drop it on to the silk, allowing it to spread out to touch the gold outline. Fill the hair freehand, using a small amount of paint so that it does not seep too far away from the gold outline. The background is also filled in freehand: paint the clouds and grass using the mint green and watered down blue paint, in thin brush strokes across the fabric.

4 Leave the paint to dry, before removing it from the frame. To fix the silk paint: place the silk painted side down on a fluffy towel, cover with a clean cloth and iron for 7 minutes on a cotton setting.

Making up the bag

1 Cut-out the three silk painted panels. Leave 1.25cm (½in) of extra fabric outside of the outer gold border line on each panel. From the white fabric, cut a rectangle 35x14cm (14x5½in), for the pocket lining. Position the panels on the lining fabric; placing them side by side, with approximately 2.5cm (1in) between the outer gold border line of each panel.

2 From the yellow bias binding cut: two lengths x 14cm (5½in) for the panel dividers, one length 35cm (14in) for the pocket top, two lengths x 35cm (14in) for the bag top, one length x 67cm (26½in) for the cord casing.

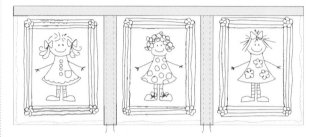

3 Pin then tack a bias binding strip between each dolly panel, then bind the top edge of the assembled pocket with a folded bias binding strip.

4 For the bag sides, cut two pink checked fabric pieces 35x31.5cm (14x12½in). Lay the pocket on the bag front. Machine stitch down the outer edges of the bias binding dividing strips: this will attach the pocket to the bag front.

5 Stitch a bias binding strip to the top edge of the front and back bag pieces.

6 Pin the front and back bag pieces together at the side seams, taking a 1.5cm seam allowance.

7 Turn the bag inside out. To form the casing for the cord: machine stitch a bias strip inside the bag, approximately 1cm (½in) down from the top edge. Sew along the top and bottom edge of the bias binding, leaving a small gap at one side for threading the cord.

8 From the yellow fabric, cut a 23.5cm (9¼in) diameter circle for the bag bottom. Working on the wrong side of the fabric, pin

then tack the circular base to the side seams. Neaten all seams. Insert the cord into the casing then tie the cord ends together.

9 To give the bag a firmer base: insert a circle of card, covered with the yellow fabric into the bottom of the bag.

To make the picture

1 Cut one piece of silk 15x8cm (6x3¼in), adding extra fabric for mounting the silk on to a frame. Trace off the small design of the three dollies on page 51, then follow the outlining and painting instructions given for the bag, on the previous page. Allow the

design to dry then iron on the reverse side to set the paint.

2 Cut a rectangle of card to fit into the frame and a piece of wadding the same size. Cut the painted fabric, adding 2.5cm (1in) to all edges.

3 Lay the wadding on to card, with the painted fabric on top. Wrap the fabric over the edges of the card, attaching to the back of the card with double sided tape.

4 Position the mounted picture into the frame and replace the back.

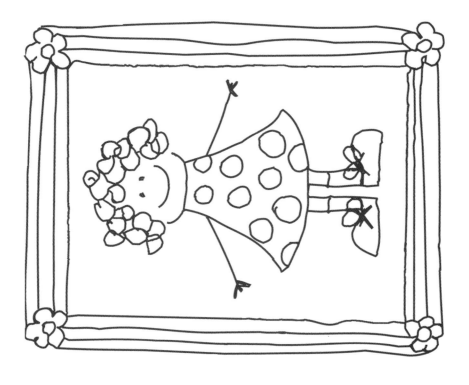

Use the individual dolly designs to make tracings for the
bag; the dolly design above is used to make the picture.

Angel Delight

Ballet angel; halo angel; candle angel and choral angel make up this delightful quartet of brightly painted cards. As you gaze at their cherub faces, you can almost hear the echo of their celestial song, as you fetch in the holly and decorate the house for Christmas

You will need

- Lightweight silk – 18x14cm (7x5½in), for each card
- Card blanks, plain front
- Silk paint – deep blue, turquoise blue, navy, mauve, raspberry pink, buttercup yellow, poppy red, fuschia pink, coral, salmon pink, lime green, bright green
- Resist outliner paste – gold
- Glitter glue – gold
- Gold stars or sequins
- Gold braid, gold spray paint
- Embroidery ring or silk painting frame, masking tape, pins
- White paper, soft pencil, paintbrush
- Gold pen, black ball-point pen
- Textured paper, scissors, kitchen paper
- Double-sided backing material, double-sided tape
- Iron, fluffy towel, clean cloth

Tracing the design

1 Cut a piece of silk large enough to take all the designs; or smaller pieces for individual cards, adding extra fabric for mounting on to a frame. Press the silk then attach it to a silk painting frame; or stretch across an embroidery ring (see Mounting and Fixing, page 8).

2 Make tracings of the angel designs on page 56 and 57 on to white paper using a soft pencil. Place the tracing, with the design facing upwards, underneath the stretched silk and secure in position with small pieces of masking tape.

3 Trace the design on to the silk, using a soft pencil. Remove the paper tracing, and re-tighten the silk if necessary.

Applying the paint

1 Use the gold resist outliner to draw over the outlines of each angel. Squeeze the tube gently keeping your hand steady, as if using an icing tube. Always keep the kitchen paper to hand and whenever you stop, wipe the nozzle and replace the cap. Take care to keep the lines continuous as any gaps will allow the paint to seep through. Leave to dry for 3-4 hours.

2 When using silk paint, drop a small amount of paint on to the fabric with a fine paintbrush. The paint will spread out to the

resist lines, then stop. Add more paint until the area is filled completely with colour.

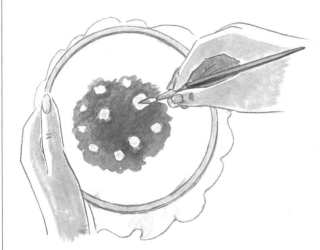

3 If you wish to make lighter spots on the paint: touch the wet paint with a clean damp paintbrush. The paintbrush will soak-up some of the paint, while making a water spot in the paint.

Painting the ballet angel

1 Using the bright blue paint fill in the sky area behind the ballet angel. Touch the wet paint with a clean damp paintbrush, making lighter marks in the paint.

2 Paint the dress lime green, adding bright green to the hem and the cloud. Use buttercup yellow to paint the wings; coral for the hair and poppy red for the ballet shoes. Paint the flesh salmon pink. Dot a clean damp paintbrush on to the cloud and the hem of the dress.

3 Make dots with the glitter glue over the wings and dress. Leave to dry then remove the painted fabric from the frame or hoop.

4 Iron fix the paint then mount the design, following the instructions on the next page.

5 Dampen the edges of the textured paper, then tear it just smaller than the size of the card. Glue the textured paper then the angel design to the turquoise card. Glue a large star on to the textured paper and a small star on the angel's hair. Make dots for the eyes, nose and mouth, carefully using a black ball-point pen.

Painting the halo angel

1 Paint the sky behind the angel bright blue, then touch the wet paint with a clean damp brush.

2 Use lime green to paint the wings; Christmas trees on the border and alternate stripes on the socks. Paint the flesh using salmon pink.

3 Paint the hair, alternate sock stripes and stars in buttercup yellow; the moons in the border, the heart, shoes and collar in poppy red; the apron and the border stars in raspberry pink; and dress in mauve. Mark water spots on the dress with a damp clean paintbrush.

4 The border background is achieved by painting wet-on-wet. Using a wet clean

brush, dampen the border area, then drop deep blue and mauve paint next to each other so they merge together. Work quickly while the paint is still wet. Leave to dry, then remove the painted fabric from the frame or hoop.

5 Iron fix then mount the design following the instructions on the next page.

6 Spray a mauve card with gold spray paint and allow to dry. Glue the mounted design on to the front of the card. Glue small gold stars to the blue background. Make dots for the eyes, nose and mouth, carefully using a black ball-point pen.

Painting the candle angel

1 Paint the sky using the turquoise blue and the candle flame, socks and wings with the buttercup yellow.

2 Paint the dress and shoes mauve, then touch the wet paint with a clean damp paintbrush to make water spots. Clean the paintbrush thoroughly then use it to remove some of the colour from the hem of the dress and the sleeve bands.

3 Paint the hair using coral; raspberry pink on the apron and fuschia pink on the edge. Fill in the flesh areas with salmon pink.

4 The border is filled in using the same colour as in the design. Dot gold glitter glue over the sky area. Leave to dry, then remove the painted fabric from the frame or hoop.

5 Iron fix then mount the design following the instructions below. Glue gold braid to the back outer edge of the design, then attach to a green card with double-sided tape. Draw around the outer edge of the card with a gold felt-tipped pen. Make dots for the eyes, nose and mouth carefully, using a black ball-point pen.

Painting the choral angel

1 Use raspberry pink to paint the bodice and the middle skirt band. Paint the main of the skirt with diluted mauve paint and the hair in buttercup yellow.

2 Dilute the raspberry pink to make pale pink then paint the wings and cloud. Use salmon pink to paint the flesh.

3 Paint the background navy, then apply gold glitter glue randomly. Leave to dry then remove the painted fabric from the frame or hoop.

4 Iron fix then mount the design following the instructions below. Attach the design to a red card using double-sided tape. Glue a star to the angel's hair, and add the features with a black ball-point pen.

5 Using a gold felt-tipped pen and glitter glue, paint notes and dots over the red card background.

Fixing and mounting the design

1 Cover the painted silk with a clean cloth and iron on a cotton setting for approximately 7 minutes to fix the colours.

2 Iron the painted and fixed fabric on to double-sided backing material.

3 Cut a piece of thin card just larger than the design. Peel off the covering on the double-sided backing material and press the design on the cartridge paper. Cover with a cloth and press with a warm iron, then cut out the design on the outer gold resist line. Mount each design on to a greetings card, following the project instructions given for each angel.

Use these designs to create your own angel cards.

Ballet Angel

Halo Angel

Choral Angel

Candle Angel

Topiary Tree

Reminiscent of Edwardian embroidery; these topiary tree designs have
been stamped using silk paint, creating a very unusual finish. Mounted in
this elegant gold dressing table set, you can be sure that you are making
a family heirloom to be used and enjoyed for years to come

Fabric requirements and design layouts should
be adapted to suit the size and shape of your
dressing table set.

You will need

- Dressing table set – mirror, brushes, tray, box
- Medium-weight silk – 50x56cm (20x22in)
- Lace – 1cm (³⁄₈in)
- Silk paint – cinnamon, meadow green, moss green
- Resist outliner paste – clear, gold
- Embroidery ring or silk painting frame, masking
  tape, pins
- Rubber eraser, synthetic washing-up sponge
- White paper, soft pencil, scissors, thick card
- Fine waterproof marker pen
- Wallpaper paste (powder),
- Craft knife, teaspoon, double-sided tape
- Flat dish for mixing paint, small paintbrush
- Container of clean water, kitchen paper
- Iron, fluffy towel, clean cotton cloth

Making the stamps

1 Make a tracing of the bush circles, bird, pot
and leaf shapes on page 61 on to white
paper, using a soft pencil. Cut out the shapes.

2 Attach the bush circles, bird and pot
tracings with a pin, to small pieces of
washing-up sponge (see Painting Techniques,
page 13). Draw around the outline of each
shape with a waterproof marker pen.

3 Use sharp scissors to cut away the sponge
from around the edge of each shape, leaving
the shape on a raised block.

4 Secure the leaf-shaped tracing to a rubber
eraser with a pin and draw around the outer
edge with waterproof marker pen.

5 Carefully cut away the background, in the
same way as the sponge but using a sharp
craft knife.

Applying the background

1 Press the silk then mount on to a frame or
embroidery hoop (see Mounting and Fixing,
page 8).

2 Lay the templates provided with your
dressing table set on to the stretched silk
fabric, and using a soft pencil, draw around the
outer edge of the design.

3 Using clear resist outliner draw a freehand lattice on to each design area, following the diagram on page 61. Squeeze the tube gently keeping your hand steady, as if using an icing tube. Always keep the kitchen paper to hand and whenever you stop, wipe the nozzle and replace the cap. If you are worried about working straight on to the silk: draw a large area of lattice on to white paper, lay it under the silk then trace over the lines with a pencil.

4 If you would prefer a plain painted background: use clear resist outliner to draw around the design area. Leave the resist to dry for 3-4 hours. Dilute the moss green paint with water and then drop a very small amount of paint on to the fabric within the design area, using the tip of the brush. The paint will spread out to the resist lines.

5 Leave the silk to dry completely before removing it from the frame or hoop.

6 To fix the silk paint: place the silk painted side down on a fluffy towel, cover with clean cloth and iron for 7 minutes on a cotton setting (see Mounting and Fixing, page 8). Wash the silk to remove the resist outliner, dry then re-iron to remove the creases.

Stamping the design

1 Stretch the silk back on to the frame. Using gold outliner, draw branches and stalks on to the fabric for stamping the leaf design, as shown in the diagram on page 61. Leave to dry.

2 Thicken each of the paint colours to be used for stamping, with wallpaper paste powder: the powder acts as a resist, thickening the paint and stopping it from spreading across the silk fabric. Use about ¹/₂ teaspoon of dry wallpaper paste to approximately 50mls of paint. Before you begin stamping, test on a spare piece of fabric. Leave the paint to dry, then wash to remove the paste mixture. If the colour washes away add more paint to the mix; if the paint bleeds across the fabric, add more paste (see Painting Techniques, page 13).

3 Load the bush sponge stamp with thickened moss green paint using a brush, then press the stamp to the fabric, refer to the main photograph on page 59; or the diagram on page 61. While the paint is still wet stamp meadow green on top. Repeat for the other bush and the bird stamp.

4 Wash out the brush in clean water, and dry on kitchen paper. Use the brush to load the pot shape stamp with thickened cinnamon coloured paint.

5 Stamp the tree trunks using the edge of a piece of thick card and cinnamon paint.

6 The leaves are stamped on to the gold lines drawn for the branches using the rubber eraser stamp and thickened moss green paint. Leave the paint to dry.

7 Apply gold resist outliner dots between the leaves to represent berries, and a gold bow on the bush.

8 On the plain fabric, use gold resist outliner to add dots to the background. Leave to dry.

Fixing the silk paint

1 Remove the fabric from the frame or hoop. Cover with a clean cotton cloth and iron on a cotton setting for approximately 7 minutes to fix the colours.

2 Gently wash the fabric to remove the paste mixture. Leave to dry then iron to remove any creases.

Assembling the set

1 Attach lace inside the metal rim of the dressing table items, using double-sided tape.

2 Cut out the painted silk on the outer pencil lines. Mount the silk on to card templates provided with the dressing table set using double-sided tape. Assemble the set following the manufacturer's instructions.

Use the designs at the top of the page to make topiary stamps; the grid should be used as a guide when drawing the background pattern, and the colour diagram to the right, shows how the stamps are used to create a design.

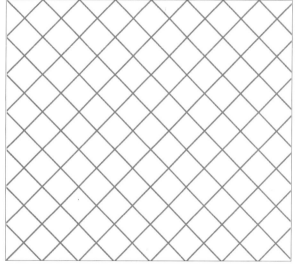

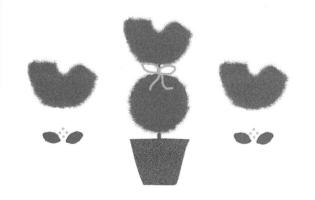

Acknowledgements

Thanks to the designers for contributing such wonderful projects:
Happy Whale (page 14), Maria Saunderson
Daisy Chain (page 20), Sandra Hardy
Sheep Scarf (page 24), Caroline Palmer
Jewelled Christmas (page 30), Sandra Hardy
Seahorse Beach Set (page 34), Caroline Palmer
Tartan Cushion and Tie-back (page 40), Annabelle Sheldrick
Glitzy Scrunch Fabric (page 44), Maria Saunderson
Dolly Bag and Picture (page 46), Sandra Hardy
Angel Delight (page 52), Maria Saunderson
Topiary Tree (page 58), Maria Saunderson

Many thanks to Ashton James and Jon Stone for their inspirational photography;
Doreen Holland for using her considerable needlework skills to make up projects;
and Penny Daw for the loan of her antique dressmaker's dummy.

Suppliers

Bostik Ltd
Ulverscroft Road
Leicester LE4 6BW
Tel: 0116 251 0015
Telephone for your local retail stockist
(Glitter glue)

Canopia
PO Box 420
Uxbridge
Middlesex UB8 2GW
Tel: 01895 235005
Mail order service
(Trinket box, picture frames)

Craft Creations Ltd
Ingersoll House
Delamare Road
Cheshunt
Herts EN8 9ND
Tel: 01922 781900
Mail order service
(Card blanks)

Craft World (Head office only)
No 8 North Street, Guildford
Surrey GU1 4AF
Tel: 07000 757070
Retail shops nationwide, telephone for local
store
(Craft warehouse)

Dylon International Ltd
Worsley Bridge Road
Lower Sydenham
London SE26 5HD
Tel: 0181 663 4296
Telephone for your local retail stockist
(Fabric paint)

Framecraft Miniatures Ltd
372-376 Summer Lane
Hockley
Birmingham
B19 3QA
Tel: 0121 212 0551
Retail shops nationwide, telephone for local
store
(Dressing table set, card blanks)

Hobby Crafts (Head office only)
River Court
Southern Sector
Bournemouth International Airport
Christchurch
Dorset BH23 6SE
Tel: 0800 272387 freephone
Retail shops nationwide, telephone for local
store
(Craft warehouse)

Home Crafts Direct
PO Box 38
Leicester
LE1 9BU
Tel: 0116 251 3139
Mail order service
(Craft equipment)

Seta Silk Paints (Distributor – office address
only)
Philip and Tacey Ltd
North Way
Andover
Hampshire
SP10 5BA
Tel: 01264 332171
Telephone for your local retail stockist
(Silk paint, outliner paste)

Index